Table of Contents

chapter One: all About donut 6

What are Donuts? 6

Essential Ingredients for Making Donuts 7

Tips for Making Donuts 8

Essential Equipment for Making Donuts 12

Chapter Two: Baked Donut Recipes 14

Delicious Sugar Lemon Donuts 14

Raspberry Glazed Donuts 17

Sweet Red Velvet Donuts 21

Cinnamon Sugar, Gluten-Free Donuts 23

Yummy Cinnamon Sugar Donuts 26

Pumpkin Donuts with Streusel Topping 29

Chocolate Glazed Caramel Drizzled Donuts 33

Sweet Cream Glazed Oreo Donuts 37

Vanilla Glazed Donuts 41

Homemade Churro Donuts 44

Vanilla Glazed Chocolate Donuts 47

Fruity Vanilla Donuts 50

Lemon Glazed Donuts 53

Chapter Three: Fried Donut Recipes 56

Delicious Bread flour Donuts 56

Crispy and Soft Donuts 59

Traditional Italian Donuts (Frittelle) 62

Bread Maker Delicious Donuts 65

Herman Sourdough Applesauce Donuts 67

Sugar Coated Sufganiot 70

Sweet French Donuts (Bugnes Moelleuses) 73

Sugar Glazed Donuts 76

Pumpkin Cranberry Jelly Donuts (Sufganiot) 79

Thera's Canadian Donuts 83

Vanilla Glazed Creamy Donuts..86

Jelly Filled Yummy Donuts 90

Costas French Donuts (Beignets).......................................93

Sweet Donuts with Apple Cider...96

Portuguese Delicious Donuts (Malasadas Dois)...............99

Quick & Easy Ricotta Donuts 102

Sugar Glazed Super Soft Donuts 105

CHAPTER ONE: ALL ABOUT DONUT

What are Donuts?

Donuts are fried or baked rounds or globules of sugared dough that is either chemically leavened or yeast-leavened. The dough is mixed and molded, placed in hot oil and fried (or spooned into the pans and baked), and glazed. Donuts filled with jam are called bismarks. Donut batter can include lemon, chocolate, or fruits such as raspberries, nuts, or raisins. Chemically-leavened donuts are made with baking powder and are usually dense and like cake. They are straightforward and quick to make. Yeast donuts are leavened when carbon dioxide is created as a result of the fermentation of yeast. These donuts are lighter in texture than chemically leavened donuts. You can easily make these sweet treats at home with basic ingredients and you don't need special equipment.

Grocery stores, privately run bakeries and franchises bake and sell donuts by making use of a pre-packed mix and carefully-controlled production. Large commercial bakeries are making thousands of dozen of donuts on a daily basis, which are being packaged and distributed across the vast regions. Donut is a favorite American snack, and as a result, donut franchises have thrived in the USA since the 1930s.

Essential Ingredients for Making Donuts

Donuts ingredients are varied; It depends on whether they're chemically or yeast-leavened. Also, ingredients for homemade donuts usually are fewer than those made from pre-packaged mixes or commercially-produced. Chemically-raised donuts make use of ingredients that include baking powder, flour, salt, liquid, and varying amounts of shortening, sugar, milk, eggs, and other flavorings. Baking powder is being used in this type of donut to leaven the dough. Ingredients such as flour, sugar, shortening, salt, milk, egg whites, yeast, water, eggs, and flavoring are used in making yeast-leavened donuts.

Donuts make in hygienic baking conditions in bakeries, franchises or grocery stores are often from pre-packaged mixes. The mixes vary but can include: flour (soy or wheat flour), milk solids, egg yolks, yeast dough conditioners, sugar, shortening, and artificial flavors. The bakeries will be required to add fresh wet ingredients such as water, eggs, and milk in the mixing process. Oil such as vegetable oil is also required for frying donuts. Frostings and glazes are often required in the donuts, whether fried or baked, and these are made with sugar, shortening, and flavoring.

Tips for Making Donuts

Baking Tips

- It is important to spray donut pans with non-stick cooking spray before pouring the batter so the donuts can be easy to remove.

- To fill the donut pan, spoon the batter into each cavity or fill a large ziplock bag with the batter. Then, cut a corner off the bag base and pipe the batter into the cavities, filling each ¾ way full.

- The donuts usually puff up when baking; filling each donut pan's cavity ¾ full is the way to go to avoid overflowing.

- The donuts are done in the oven once they have turned golden brown and use insert toothpick and it comes out without any stain.

Frying tips

- Drop a small piece of dough into the oil to test if it's hot. If the dough does not start frying immediately, the oil is still cold and if it browns too quickly, that means the oil is too hot, so reduce the heat.

- Place a batch of the donut into the hot oil and continue to shape the remaining. The ideal thing is to have another person doing the frying while one person is doing the shaping because doing both tasks together is just no easy, as the dough is so sticky.

Homemade donuts are somewhat of a project, but the tasks are less than what you may think of, and the result is a really delightful, hot, crispy donuts. Once you have mastered the basic recipes for a soft, yeasted donut, you can do any kinds of fillings, glazes, and toppings you like.

In any dough recipe, the right balance of dry and wet ingredients is vital. Make sure the ingredients are correctly measured. Use a spoon to stir your flour before spooning it into a dry measuring cup. Don't push a measuring cup into a flour bin; doing so can lead to 25 percent more flour than required, which will automatically lead to dense donuts.

To test if donuts have raised enough, after cutting them out, use a fingertip to touch them; if they spring back quickly, give them more time; if they spring back slowly, they're adequately proofed. If they don't spring back at all, that means they have over-proofed.

In addition, it is important to let your dough proof in a warm environment (but not above 110 degrees F) so, you don't deactivate the yeast that will allow the donuts to rise properly.

Storing Tips

Refrigerate: Leave the donuts in the rack to cool completely and then place them at room temperature in an airtight container with a paper towel to soak up excess moisture for about three days. Then, place in the refrigerator for up to 7 days.

Freeze: To freeze, wrap the donuts in foil or plastic wrap and then place them in a freezer bag.

To serve, thaw the donuts at room temperature and warm them in an oven or microwave.

Essential Equipment for Making Donuts

- Paring Knife: Running paring knife around the edge of donut and pan after baking makes for easy removal.

- Measuring Spoon and Measuring Cup

- Mixers: A hand mixer is suitable for frosting and whipping creams

- Mini Donut/ Donut Hole Maker; for making donut hole

- Heavy Skillet, Deep-fryer or Large Saucepan for frying donuts

- Parchment Paper

- Wire Rack or Paper Towels

- Donut cutter; for cutting donuts

- Rolling Pin: A metal or wood rolling pin is used to roll out yeast-based donuts before cutting it into a ring or round shapes.

- Plastic wrap: This can be used to cover the dough while sits do rise.

- Pastry Bags: This is used for piping donut batter into a baking pan before baking.

- Spatulas and Whisks: These are used to combine wet and dry ingredients. You can use a rubber spatula to scrape batter from the sides of the bowls.

- Kitchen Scale

- Donut Baking Pans

- Baking sheet

- Oven for baking

- Mixing bowl

CHAPTER TWO: BAKED DONUT RECIPES

Delicious Sugar Lemon Donuts

Sugar Lemon Baked Donuts are soft, citrusy, and generously coated in a crispy, infused sugar lemon-zest. This recipe is excellent for dessert or breakfast treat!

Total Time: 30 minutes

Servings: 12

Yield: 12 donuts

Ingredients:

- 13/4 cups of all-purpose flour
- 1/4 cup of cornstarch
- 2 tsp of baking powder
- 3/4 cup of sugar
- 1 tsp of salt

- 2 eggs
- 3/4 cup of buttermilk
- 2 tbsp. of butter, melted
- ½ tsp of pure vanilla extract
- 1 tbsp. of freshly-squeezed lemon juice
- 2 tsp of grated lemon zest
- For the Coating:
- 1/2 cup of sugar
- 4 tsp of grated lemon zest
- 6 tbsp. of butter, melted

Directions:

- Step one: Preheat oven to 350° F and lightly spray two 6-count donut pans with a non-stick cooking spray; set aside.
- Step two: Combine flour and cornstarch in a large bowl. Add baking powder, sugar, and salt; stir until well combined. Next, whisk in the egg, buttermilk,

vanilla, lemon juice, and lemon zest until the mixture is well combined and pourable.

- Step three: spoon the batter into the donut pans, filling each cavity about ¾ full.

- Step four: Place the donut pans inside the preheated oven and bake for 15 minutes until the donuts are golden brown. Let sit the in pans for 5 minutes to cool. Next, run a knife around the donuts, remove them from the pans and then put them on a baking sheet or wire rack.

To prepare the coating: Blend the sugar and lemon zest in a mini food processor until very smooth, or if you don't have a food processor, you can stir the two ingredients to combine. Next, put the butter in a shallow bowl. To serve, dip a side of each donut in the melted butter while still warm. Then press into the sugar mixture. Enjoy!

Nutritional fact per serving: Calories: 246kcal; Carbohydrates: 39g; Protein: 3g; Cholesterol: 49mg; Fat: 9g; Saturated Fat: 5g; Sodium: 288mg; Calcium: 56mg; Potassium: 117mg; Fiber: 1g; Sugar: 22g; Vitamin A: 300IU; Vitamin C: 1.7mg; Iron: 1mg.

Raspberry Glazed Donuts

These super easy to make raspberry baked donuts with glazed raspberry are naturally pink without food coloring and are packed with berry flavor!

Total time 20 minutes

Servings: 8

Yield: 8 donuts

Ingredients:

For Raspberry purée:

- 1 1/2 cups of fresh raspberry
- 2 tbsp. of sugar
- Raspberry Donuts:
- 3/4 cups of old fashioned oats
- 1/4 cup of freeze-dried raspberries
- 1/4 cup of all-purpose flour
- 1/4 cup of granulated sugar
- 1/4 tsp of baking soda

- 1 tsp of baking powder
- 1/2 tsp of salt
- 2 tbsp. of butter or coconut oil, melted
- 2 tbsp. of honey
- 1/4 cup of almond milk
- 1/4 cup of raspberry puree
- 1 tsp of pure vanilla extract
- 1 egg, beaten

For Glaze:

2 tbsp. of raspberry puree

1 cup of powdered sugar

Directions:

- Step one: Preheat oven to 350° F and spray the donut pan with a non-stick cooking spray; set aside.
- Step two: Place the oats, freeze-dried raspberries, and flour in your mixer bowl. Next, run the mixer, starting at low speed and increasing to high, for about one minute until the mixture is very smooth and the color

is light pink. Then, transfer the mixture to a medium bowl.

- Step two: Add the granulated sugar, baking soda, baking powder, and salt to the flour mixture. Mix thoroughly until combined well and set aside. Then, rinse your mixer bowl.

- Step three: Make raspberry Purée: Run 11/2 cup of raspberries and 2 tbsp. of sugar in a blender for about 2 minutes or until very smooth. Next, transfer the raspberry purée to a small bowl and set aside.

- Step four: Add the butter or coconut oil, almond milk, honey, vanilla extract, and raspberry purée to the mixer bowl. Then, blend the mixture for about 1 minute or until it is very smooth. Add half of the flour mixture to the wet ingredients in the mixer bowl and blend to combine. Next, add the remaining half of the flour mixture and blend until the mixture is very smooth. Lastly, add the beaten egg and blend until the batter is well combined and pourable.

- Step five: spoon or pipe the batter into the donut pans, filling each cavity about ¾ full.

- Step six: Place the donut pan inside the preheated oven and bake for 15 minutes until the donuts are golden brown. Let sit the in pan for 5 minutes to cool. Next, run a knife around the donuts, remove them from the pan and then put them on a baking sheet or wire rack.

To prepare the raspberry glaze, combine 1 cup powdered sugar and 2 tablespoons of raspberry purée; stir the mixture until smooth. To serve, spoon about 2 tbsp. of glaze on top of each donut while still warm. Top the donuts with dried raspberries or sprinkles if desired. Allow the glazed donuts to harden before you eat. Enjoy!

Nutrition fact per serving: Calories: 134.3kcal; Protein: 2.4g; Fat: 5g; Potassium: 57.2mg; Carbohydrates: 21g; Fiber: 2.5g; Vitamin A: 85IU; Vitamin C: 8mg; Sugar: 11.6g; Calcium: 22mg; Iron: 0.7mg.

Sweet Red Velvet Donuts

Total time: 20 minutes

Servings; 12

Yield: 12 donuts

Ingredients;

- 2 cups of all-purpose flour
- 1/2 cup of red cocoa powder
- 1 tsp of baking powder
- 1/2 tsp of salt
- 2 cups of sugar
- 1/2 cup of unsalted butter
- 2 tsp of vanilla extract
- 2 eggs, beaten
- 1 cup of buttermilk
- 2 drops or more of red food coloring, optional

Directions:

- Step one: Preheat oven to 350° F and lightly spray two 6-count donut pans with a non-stick cooking spray; set aside.

- Step two: Combine the flour, baking powder, cocoa powder, and salt in a large bowl. Combine sugar and butter in a mixer on medium-high speed for 3 minutes or until light and smooth. Next, add the vanilla extract, mix for 30 seconds, add the egg, mix for another 30 seconds. Turn the mixer off and scrape the down-sides. Run the mixer on high speed for about 20 seconds. Then, reduce speed to low; add 1/2 of the flour mixture and then buttermilk; add the remaining flour mixture. Lastly, if using, add red food coloring. Mix until well combined and pourable.

- Step three: Spoon or pipe the batter into the donut pans, filling each cavity about ¾ full.

- Step four: Place the donut pans inside the preheated oven and bake for 15 minutes until the donuts are golden brown. Let sit the in pans for 5 minutes to cool. Next, run a knife around the donuts, remove them from the pans and then put them on a baking sheet or wire rack.

Cinnamon Sugar, Gluten-Free Donuts

Total time: 40 minutes

Serving: 12

Yield; 12 donuts

Ingredients:

- 1/3 cup of melted unsalted butter or refined coconut oil
- 3/4 cup of granulated sugar
- 1/3 cup of bean flour
- 3/4 cup of brown rice flour
- 1/4 cup of arrowroot
- 1/2 cup of potato starch
- 1/2 tsp of xanthan gum
- 11/2 tsp baking powder
- 1/4 tsp of baking soda
- 1/2 tsp of salt

- 1/4 cup of vanilla extract

- 6 tbsp. of unsweetened applesauce

- Cinnamon sugar, for sprinkling, optional

Directions:

- Step one: Preheat oven to 350° F and spray two 6-count donut pans with a non-stick cooking spray; set aside.

- Step two: Combine the sugar, bean flour, rice flour, arrowroot, potato starch, xanthan gum, baking powder, baking soda, and salt in a large bowl. Next, stir in the butter or oil, vanilla, applesauce, and hot water; stir the mixture using a rubber spatula until well combined, being careful not to over mix. Scoop 2½ tbsp. of the batter into each mold of donut and use a toothpick to spread evenly around.

- Step three: Place the donut pans inside the preheated oven and bake for 15, until the donuts are golden brown. Let sit the in molds for 5 minutes to cool. Next, run a knife around the donuts, remove them from the pans and then put them on a baking sheet.

- Step four: Sprinkle the donuts with cinnamon sugar while still warm and serve. Enjoy?

Nutritional analysis per serving: 203 calories; 5 grams saturated fat; 6 grams fat; 1 gram protein; 34 grams carbohydrates; 132 milligrams sodium; 18 grams sugars; 1 gram dietary fiber

Yummy Cinnamon Sugar Donuts

Cinnamon sugar baked donuts are very delicious, easy, and quick to make and coat with cinnamon sugar.

Total Time: 25 minutes

Servings: 12

Yield: 12 Donuts

Ingredients:

- 2 cups of all-purpose flour
- 1 ½ cups of sugar
- ½ teaspoon of salt
- 1 tsp of cinnamon
- 1 egg
- 2 teaspoons of baking powder
- 1 1/4 cups of whole milk
- 2 tbsp. of butter melted
- 1 tbsp. of vanilla

- For topping:
- ½ cup of butter melted
- ½ teaspoon of cinnamon
- ½ cup of sugar

Directions:

- Step one: Preheat oven to 350° F and spray two 6-count donut pans with a non-stick cooking spray.
- Step two: Combine all the dry ingredients in a large bowl and set aside. Next, in a separate bowl, combine the wet ingredients; slowly stir the mixture over the dry ingredients and then mix until well combined and pourable.
- Step three: Spoon or pipe the batter into the donut pans, filling each cavity about ¾ full.
- Step four: Place the donut pans inside the preheated oven and bake for 15 minutes until the donuts are golden brown. Let sit the in pans for 5 minutes to cool. Next, run a knife around the donuts, remove them from the pans and then put them on a baking sheet.

- Step five: Combine the butter, cinnamon, and sugar. Next, lightly dip the donuts in the cinnamon mixture while still warm. Enjoy!

- Lightly dip each donut in butter, followed by cinnamon and sugar mixture, and serve warm.

Nutrition fact per serving: Calories:315kcal; Carbohydrates:51g; Sodium:199mg; Protein:4g; Fat:11g; Saturated Fat:7g; Potassium:128mg; Fiber:1g; Calcium:67mg; Sugar:35g; Vitamin A:356IU; Iron:1mg; Cholesterol:42mg.

Pumpkin Donuts with Streusel Topping

Total time: 25 minutes

Serving: 6

Yield: 6 donuts

Ingredients:

For Donuts:

- 1/2 cup of granulated sugar
- 1/4 cup of unsalted butter, softened
- 1/2 tsp of vanilla extract
- 1 large egg, beaten
- 1/2 cup of pumpkin purees (not pie filling)
- 1 cup of all-purpose flour
- 1/2 tsp of baking soda
- 1/2 tsp of baking powder
- 1/4 tsp of kosher salt
- 2 tsp of ground cinnamon

- 1/2 tsp of ground ginger
- 1/2 tsp of ground nutmeg
- 1/2 tsp of ground cloves

For Streusel: ☐

- ½ cup of light brown sugar, packed
- 1 teaspoon of ground cinnamon
- ½ cup of all-purpose flour
- 2 tablespoons unsalted butter, melted

For Glaze:

- 1-2 tbsp. of milk
- 1 cup powdered sugar
- 1 teaspoon of cinnamon

Directions:

- Step one: Preheat oven to 350° F and lightly spray two 6-count donut pans with a non-stick cooking spray; set aside.

- Step two: Combine sugar and butter in a small mixing bowl until creamy. Stir in vanilla and egg; mix until well combined. Next, stir in the pumpkin puree and then add the flour, baking soda, baking powder, salt, and spices. Mix thoroughly until well combined.

- Step three: spoon the batter into the donut pans, filling each cavity about ¾ full.

- Step four: Combine the streusel ingredients in a small bowl and sprinkle it over the pumpkin batter inside the pan. Next, press the streusel gently to the top of the batter.

- Step four: Place the donut pans inside the preheated oven and bake for 15 minutes until the donuts are golden brown. Let sit the in pans for 5 minutes to cool. Next, run a knife around the donuts, remove them from the pans and then put them on a baking sheet or wire rack.

- Combine all the ingredients for the glaze in a shallow bowl until very smooth. To serve, dip each donut inside the glaze while still warm. Enjoy!

Nutrition facts per serving: Calories:438; Trans Fat: 0g; Saturated Fat: 8g; Unsaturated Fat: 4g; Total Fat: 13g;

Cholesterol: 62mg; Sodium: 266mg; Carbohydrates: 78g; Fiber: 2g; Sugar: 50g; Protein: 5g.

Chocolate Glazed Caramel Drizzled Donuts

These Chocolate Glazed Sweet Caramel Drizzled Donuts recipes are sprinkled with toasted pecans. A mouth-watering breakfast or dessert that tastes great!

Total Time: 40 minutes

Servings: 12

Yield: 12 donuts

Ingredients:

For Donuts:

- 2 3/4 cups of all-purpose flour
- 1 cup of sugar
- 1 1/2 tsp of baking soda
- 2 tsp of baking powder
- 1 1/2 tsp of salt
- 1 1/2 cup of sour cream

- 3 tbsp. of butter, melted
- 3 eggs, beaten

For Chocolate Glaze:

- 8 oz. of milk chocolate finely chopped
- 1/4 cup of heavy cream
- 2 tbsp. of butter
- 2 tbsp. of corn syrup

For Caramel Drizzle:

- 10 caramels
- 2 tbsp. of heavy cream
- 1/3 cup of chopped pecans toasted

Directions:

- Step one: Preheat oven to 350° F and lightly spray two 6-count donut pans with a non-stick cooking spray; set aside.
- Step two: Combine the flour, sugar, baking soda, baking powder, and salt in a large bowl. Stir together the sour cream, butter, and egg in a medium mixing

bowl. Next, stir in the wet ingredients to the dry ingredients. Mix thoroughly until well combined and pourable.

- Step three: Spoon or pipe the batter into the donut pans, filling each cavity about ¾ full.

- Step four: Place the donut pans inside the preheated oven and bake for 15 minutes until the donuts are golden brown. Let sit the in pans for 5 minutes to cool. Next, run a knife around the donuts, remove them from the pans and then put them on a baking sheet or wire rack.

To prepare chocolate glaze, combine the chocolate glaze ingredients in a heat-proof bowl and microwave for 1 minute, occasionally stirring until the mixture combined.

To prepare caramel drizzle, combine the caramel and heavy cream and microwave for 30 seconds. Let the caramel mixture sits to cool a bit.

To serve, dip each donut in the glaze while still warm. Then, spoon the caramel drizzle on top of the donuts. Top with the chopped pecans and Enjoy!

Nutrition Facts per serving: Calories 467 Calories from Fat 207% Daily Value; Cholesterol 79mg26%; Fat 23g35%; Carbohydrates 61g20%; Saturated Fat 12g75%; Sodium 537mg23%; Potassium 242mg7%; Protein 6g12%; Fiber 2g8%; Sugar 35g39%; Vitamin A 495IU10%; Calcium 95mg10%; Vitamin C 0.2mg0%; Iron 2.2mg12

Sweet Cream Glazed Oreo Donuts

These are perfect baked chocolate donuts studded with Oreo. Glazed with sweet cream cheese and sprinkled with crumbled cookies. These make another perfect breakfast treat!

Total time: 25 minutes

Servings: 10

Yield: 10 donuts

Ingredients:

- 1 cup of all-purpose flour
- 1/3 cup of cocoa powder
- 1/2 cup of packed light brown sugar
- 1/2 tsp of salt
- 1/2 tsp of baking soda
- 3/4 tsp of baking powder
- 1/2 cup of milk
- 1 large egg, beaten

- 1 1/2 tsp of vanilla extract

- 1/4 cup of vegetable oil or melted coconut oil

- 6 Oreo cookies crushed into crumbs

- Cream Cheese Frosting

- 2 tbsp. of unsalted butter, melted

- 4 oz. of cream cheese, softened

- 1 1/2 tsp of vanilla extract or vanilla bean paste

- 3 tbsp. of milk

- 2 cups powdered sugar

- 4 Oreo cookies crushed into crumbs

Directions:

- Step one: Preheat oven to 350° F and spray two 6-count donut pans with a non-stick cooking spray; set aside.

- Step two: Combine the flour, cocoa powder, brown sugar, salt, baking soda, and baking powder in a large bowl. Mix thoroughly until well combined. Set aside

- Step three: Combine the milk, egg, vanilla extract, and coconut oil in a medium bowl. Next, slowly stir in the milk mixture into dry ingredients, stirring until combine well. At this point, the batter will very thick. Slowly fold in the crushed cookies to the flour mixture.

- Step four: spoon or pipe the batter into the donut pans, filling each cavity about ¾ full.

- Step five: Place the donut pans inside the preheated oven and bake for 15 minutes until the donuts are golden brown. Let sit the in pans for 5 minutes to cool. Next, run a knife around the donuts, remove them from the pans and then put them on a baking sheet or wire rack.

For the cream cheese frosting, whisk together the butter and cream cheese until very smooth. Next, combine vanilla extract, milk, and sugar. Stir well until it reaches the consistency that you like. If needed, add more powdered sugar and milk.

To serve, dip each donut halfway into the frosting and sprinkle with the crushed Oreo cookies. Enjoy!

Nutrition fact per serving: Calories: 370kcal; Potassium: 170mg; Carbohydrates: 56g; Fat: 15g; Cholesterol: Protein: 4g; 36mg; Sodium: 280mg; Fiber: 2g; Sugar: 41g; Vitamin A: 266IU; Calcium: Potassium: 170mg; 61mg; Iron: 2mg

Vanilla Glazed Donuts

The super soft and yummy baked donuts dipped in a thick vanilla glaze and then topped with sprinkles.

Total time: 20 minutes

Yield: 6 donuts

Servings: 6

Ingredients:

For Donuts:

- 1 cup of all-purpose flour
- 1 tsp of baking powder
- 1/3 cup of granulated sugar
- 1/2 tsp of salt
- 2 tbsp. of unsalted butter, melted and cooled
- 1/3 cup+1 1/2 tbsp. of milk
- 1 egg, beaten
- 1 tsp of vanilla extract

For Vanilla Glaze:

- 1 or 2 tbsp. of milk
- 1/2 tsp of vanilla extract
- 1/2 cup of powdered sugar
- A pinch of salt
- Food coloring and sprinkles, optional

Directions:

- Step one: Preheat oven to 350° F and lightly spray a 6-count donut pan with a non-stick cooking spray; set aside.
- Step two: Combine the flour, sugar, salt, and baking powder in a large bowl. Mix the milk, egg, vanilla extract, and melted butter in a separate bowl.
- Step three: Slowly stir in the flour mixture to the wet ingredients until very smooth and pourable batter. Next, spoon or pipe the batter into the donut pans, filling each cavity about ¾ full.
- Step four: Place the donut pan inside the preheated oven and bake for 15 minutes until the donuts are

golden brown. Let sit in the pan for 5 minutes to cool. Next, run a knife around the donuts, remove them from the pan and then put them on a baking sheet or wire rack.

To prepare the glaze, combine vanilla extract, sugar, and salt in a medium bowl. Add 1 tbsp. of milk; stir well until it reaches your desired consistency. Then, if desired, add food coloring.

To serve, dip donuts in the vanilla glaze while still warm and then return to the rack. Top with sprinkle immediately. Let the donuts sit for about 30 minutes for the glaze to set at room temperature before serving. Enjoy!

Homemade Churro Donuts

The easy to make Homemade Baked Churro Donuts recipe is a crush up of two favorite desserts that taste great when combined.

Total Time: 50 minutes

Servings: 12

Yield: 12 donuts

Ingredients:

- 2 cups of all-purpose flour
- 1/2 tsp of cinnamon
- 1/3 cup of sugar
- 1 tsp of baking powder
- 1/4 tsp of salt
- 1 1/3 cup of milk
- 3 eggs, beaten
- 1 tsp of vanilla extract
- 1/2 cup of butter, melted

For Churro Topping:

- 1/4 cup of butter melted
- 1/2 cup of sugar
- 2 tbsp. of cinnamon
- For the Chocolate Sauce:
- 1/2 cup of chocolate chopped
- 2 tbsp. of cream

Directions:

- Step one: Preheat oven to 350° F and lightly spray two 6-count donut pans with a non-stick cooking spray; set aside.
- Step two: Combine the flour, cinnamon, sugar, salt, and baking powder in a large bowl. Mix the milk, egg, vanilla, and melted butter in a separate bowl.
- Step three: Slowly stir in the flour mixture to the wet ingredients until very smooth and pourable. Next, spoon or pipe the batter into the donut pans, filling each cavity about ¾ full.

- Step four: Place the donut pans inside the preheated oven and bake for 15 minutes until the donuts are golden brown. Let sit the in pans for 5 minutes to cool. Next, run a knife around the donuts +and remove them from the pans and then put them on a baking sheet or wire rack.

To make the topping, melt ¼ cup of butter in a small shallow bowl. Next, combine sugar and cinnamon in a separate small bowl, set aside.

Prepare the chocolate ganache by melting the chocolate in a microwave. Next, remove from the microwave and stir in the 2 tbsp. cream until a shiny, thick ganache is achieved.

To serve, brush each donut with the melted butter; after that, coat each side of the donuts completely with the cinnamon mixture. Next, dip the top side of each donut generously in the chocolate ganache. Enjoy!

Vanilla Glazed Chocolate Donuts

The classic baked Vanilla Glazed chocolate donuts recipes make a perfect, easy weekend breakfast treat!

Total Time: 35 minutes

Servings: 7

Yield: About 8 donuts

Ingredients:

- 1 cup of all-purpose flour
- ⅓ Cup of cocoa powder
- ¼ cup of granulated sugar
- ½ cup of brown sugar
- ½ tsp of baking soda
- ¼ tsp of salt
- ½ tsp of espresso powder to bring out the chocolate flavor
- 1 egg, beaten
- 6 tbsp. of half & half

- 1 tsp of vanilla extract
- 1/4 cup of sour cream
- 1 tbsp. of butter, melted

For Vanilla Glaze

- 1 cup of powdered sugar
- 3 tbsp. of whole milk
- 1/2 tsp of vanilla extract

Directions:

- Step one: Preheat oven to 350° F and spray the donut pan with a non-stick cooking spray; set aside
- Step two: Combine the 1 cup flour, 1/3 cup of cocoa powder, granulated sugar, brown sugar, baking soda, salt, and espresso powder in a large bowl. Thoroughly mix until combined well. Next, combine the half & half and egg in a small bowl. Then, make a hole in the center of the flour mixture and stir in the egg mixture. Stir until very smooth (batter would be a bit thick). Stir in the vanilla extract, sour cream, and butter; mix thoroughly until very smooth and pourable.

- Step three: spoon the batter or pipe into the donut pans, filling each cavity about ¾ full.

- Step four: Place the donut pan inside the preheated oven and bake for 8 minutes, until the donuts are golden brown. Let sit the in pan for 5 minutes to cool. Next, run a knife around the donuts, remove them from the pan and then put them on a baking sheet or wire rack.

To make the vanilla glaze: Combine 1 cup of powdered sugar, 3 tablespoons of milk, and ½ tsp of vanilla extract in a shallow bowl.

To serve: Dip each donut in the vanilla glaze and top with. Leave the glaze for about 2 minutes to harden. Enjoy!

Fruity Vanilla Donuts

Total time: 1 hour 2 minutes

Servings: 8

Yield: 8 donuts

Ingredients:

- 1 cup of milk
- 1/2 cup of fruity pebble
- 1 1/4 cups of all-purpose flour
- 3/4 cups sugar
- 1/4 tsp of nutmeg
- 1 tsp of baking powder
- 1/4 tsp of salt
- 1 egg, beaten
- 1 1/2 tsp of vanilla extract
- 1 tbsp. vegetable or canola oil
- 1 1/4 cup pow dered sugar

- 2-3 tbsp. of cereal milk
- 1/2 tsp of vanilla extract
- Fruity Pebbles for topping

Directions:

- Step one: Preheat oven to 350° F and spray the donut pan with a non-stick cooking spray. Next, in a large bowl, combine the Fruity Pebble Cereal and milk and let sit for about 20 minutes.

- Step two: Strain cereal from milk, divide the milk into two; keep 1/2 cup for the donut batter and reserve the remaining for the glaze.

- Step three: Combine 1¼ cup of flour with sugar nutmeg, salt, and baking powder in a mixing bowl. Next, stir in the beaten egg, vanilla extract, ½ cup of cereal milk, and oil. Mix thoroughly until well combined and pourable.

- Step four: Spoon or pipe the batter into the donut pans, filling each cavity about ¾ full.

- Step five: Place the donut pans inside the preheated oven and bake for 15 minutes, until the donuts are golden brown. Let sit the in molds for 5 minutes to cool. Next, run a knife around the donuts, remove them from the molds and then put them on a baking sheet or wire rack.

To make Cereal Milk Vanilla Glaze:

Combine the 11/4 cup of sugar and 2 tablespoons of the reserved cereal milk in a shallow bowl; mix well until combine. Next, stir in the vanilla extract; add more cereal milk if the glaze is too thick.

To serve, sprinkle the donuts with fruity pebbles before the glaze. This will harden the glaze and make it set before eating.

Lemon Glazed Donuts

This baked lemon donuts recipe is filled with bright lemon savor. You can top it with powdered sugar, lemon glaze, or lemon sugar.

Total time: 32 minutes

Servings: 6

Yield: 6 -7 donuts

Ingredients:

- 1 1/3 cups of all-purpose flour
- 1 tsp of baking powder
- 3/4 cup granulated sugar
- 1/4 tsp of salt
- 2 tbsp. of lemon zest
- 1 1/2 tbsp. of fresh lemon juice
- 1 egg, beaten
- 1/2 cup of buttermilk
- 1/2 tsp of vanilla extract

- 1 tbsp. of butter, melted
- Lemon Glaze:
- 1 cup powdered sugar
- 2 tsp of lemon zest, optional
- 2-3 tbsp. of fresh lemon juice

For Lemon Sugar

- 1 cup of granulated sugar
- 1 tbsp. of lemon zest
- 5 tbsp. of butter, melted

Directions

- Step one: Preheat oven to 350° F and spray 6- count donut pans with a non-stick cooking spray.
- Step two: Combine the flour, baking powder, 3/4 cup sugar, 1/4 tsp salt, and 2 tbsp. lemon zest. Next, stir in the lemon juice, beaten egg, and buttermilk. Mix thoroughly until well combined. Then, whist in vanilla extracts and butter; mix well with a spatula or your hand.

- Step three: Spoon or pipe the batter into the donut pans, filling each cavity about ¾ full.

- Step four: Place the donut pan inside the preheated oven and bake for 15 minutes until the donuts are golden brown. Let sit the in pan for 5 minutes to cool. Next, run a knife around the donuts, remove them from the pan and then put them on a baking sheet or wire rack.

To make lemon Glaze:

Combine powdered sugar, lemon juice, and lemon zest in a deep bowl and dip each donut in it while still warm.

To make lemon Sugar:

Combine the sugar and zest in a separate shallow bowl. Next, dip each donut in the melted butter while still warm. After that, dip in the lemon sugar – butter helps to hold lemon sugar with donuts.

CHAPTER THREE: FRIED DONUT RECIPES

Delicious Bread flour Donuts

Yield: 10 4-inch donuts

Total time: 13 hours, 45 minutes

Ingredients:

- 3 3/4 cups of bread flour
- 1/4 cup of sugar
- 1 tbsp. of instant yeast
- 1 tbsp. of salt
- 6 large eggs, beaten
- 2 sticks, plus 5 tbsp. of unsalted butter
- 1 1/2 cups of sugar for coating donuts
- 8 cups of vegetable oil for deep-frying

Directions:

- Step one: Add the flour, ¼ cup of sugar, yeast, and salt in a stand mixer bowl fitted with the dough hook attachment. Next, run the mixer on speed one while stirring the mixture. Pour the beaten egg and continue running the mixer on speed 1, scraping dough hook and bowl occasionally, until dough is formed approximately two minutes. Next, increase the running speed to 2; add the unsalted butter in three batches, ensuring butter is well beaten before adding another batch and scraping the dough hook and bowl as necessary, approximately ten minutes total.

- Step two: Once the dough is smooth and stretchy, transfer it to a greased large bowl. Next, cover the bowl with plastic wrap and refrigerate overnight.

- Step three: Transfer the dough to a lightly floured work surface and roll it out to a ½ inch thick with a floured rolling pin. Next, cut out 4 inch round donuts with a round donut cutter and then create a hole in the center.

- Step four: line a baking sheet with parchment paper and place the donuts on it. Next, cover the donuts loosely using a plastic wrap and let sit for 1 hour at room temperature until it rises to double.

- Step five: In a large heavy skillet, deep-fryer, or large saucepan, heat the oil to 350°F (175°C). With a wide spatula, slide a few donuts at a time into the hot oil, turning them around as they float to the top. Fry each side of donuts until golden brown. Next, remove fried donuts from hot oil and drain on a wire rack or paper towels. Coat the donuts with sugar while still warm. Enjoy!

Crispy and Soft Donuts

Total time: 2 hours 40 minutes

Serving: 18

Yield: 18 donuts

Ingredients:

- 2 (.25 oz.) packets of active dry yeast
- 1/4 cup of warm water (105 to 115 degrees)
- 1/2 cup of white sugar
- 1 1/2 cups of lukewarm milk
- 2 large eggs
- 1 tsp of salt
- 1/3 cup of shortening
- 5 cups of all-purpose flour
- 8 cups of vegetable oil for frying
- 1/3 cup of butter
- 11/2 tsp of vanilla

- 2 cups of confectioners' sugar

- 4 tbsp. of hot water or as needed

Directions:

- Step one: Sprinkle the yeast over the warm water and leave it until dissolved about five minutes.

- Step two: Combine the yeast mixture, sugar, milk, eggs, salt, shortening, 2 cups of flour in a large bowl. Stir with your hands for a few minutes. Next, stir in remaining flour, half cup a time, stirring until the dough stops sticking to the bowl. After that, knead the dough until smooth and elastic, 5 minutes. Next, transfer the dough into a greased bowl; cover the bowl loosely with a damp wrap in a warm area (at room temperature) until it rises to double.

- Step three: Transfer the dough to a floured work surface and roll out to half-inch thickness. Next, cut the dough into 18 pieces round shape with a donut cutter and leave the donuts to rise again until double.

- Step four: Place a saucepan over medium heat and melt the butter inside it. Next, stir in the vanilla and confectioners' sugar until very smooth. After that, remove the heat and stir in hot water 1 tbsp. at a time until the icing is fairly thin but not watery. Then set aside.

- Step five: In a large heavy skillet or deep-fryer, heat the oil to 350°F. With a wide spatula, slide a few donuts at a time into the hot oil, turning them around as they rise to the surface. Fry each side of donuts until golden brown. Next, remove fried donuts from hot oil and drain on a wire rack or paper towels. Then, dip donuts into the glaze when still warm. Place the donuts back into the wire racks to drain off excess. Place a tray or cookie sheet under racks for easier clean-up.

Nutrition facts per serving: 331 calories; carbohydrates 47.3g 15% DV; protein 5.3g 11% DV; cholesterol 31.3mg 10% DV; fat 13.4g 21% DV; sodium 171mg 7% DV.

Traditional Italian Donuts (Frittelle)

This fried donut recipe is light and puffy. It's absolutely delicious and great for Christmas Eve treat!

Yield: 24 Donuts

Serving 12

Ingredients:

- 2 cups of all-purpose flour
- 1 tbsp. of sugar
- 1/4 tsp of salt
- 13/4 of lukewarm water
- 3/4 tsp of dried yeast
- 1 tbsp. lemon or orange juice
- 1 tsp lemon or orange peel
- Rum-soaked raisins, optional
- 4 cups of vegetable oil for frying
- ¼ cup of sugar for dusting

Directions:

- Step one: Sprinkle the yeast over lukewarm water in a small bowl and let sit to dissolve for about 10 minutes.

- Step two: In a large bowl, combine the flour, sugar, and salt; stir the mixture to be well combined. Next, slowly stir in the yeast mixture, orange juice, and orange peel; using your hand, mix the ingredients until very smooth and firm. Then, add the rum raisins if desired. Cover the dough with a plastic wrap and let sit to rise to double.

- Step three: Transfer the dough to a floured surface and roll it out into ¼ inch thick. Next, cut the dough into round pieces (donut shape) and create a hole in the center.

- Step four: In a large heavy skillet, deep-fryer, or large saucepan, heat the oil to 350°F (175°C). With a wide spatula, slide a few donuts at a time into the hot oil, turning them around as they float to the top. Fry each side of donuts until golden brown. Next, remove fried donuts from hot oil and drain on a wire rack or paper towels. Coat the donuts with sugar while still warm. Enjoy!

Nutrition Information per serving: Calories: 50mg carbohydrates; 36 total fat; 1g saturated fat; 4g protein; 1g cholesterol; 5g fiber.

Bread Maker Delicious Donuts

Total: 1 hour 35 minutes

Servings: 16

Yield: 16 donuts

Ingredients:

- 1/2 cup of warm milk
- 1/2 beaten egg
- 1/4 cup of butter
- 2 cups of all-purpose flour
- 1 tsp of salt
- 1/4 cup of white sugar
- 1 tsp of active dry yeast
- 6 cups of vegetable oil for frying

Directions

- Step one: Add the egg and milk into the pan of your automatic bread machine. Next, add the butter, flour, salt, sugar, and yeast in that order so the yeast will be on top. Select the dough setting and then start the machine.

- Step two: Once the dough circle is completed, transfer the dough to the floured surface. Next, knead the dough until smooth and elastic. Roll out the dough into 1/4-inch-thick and then cut into 6 pieces round shape with a floured donut cutter and then create a hole in the center with a small cutter. Cover the donuts with a plastic wrap and let sit for about 40 minutes to rise.

- Step three: In a large heavy skillet, deep-fryer, or large saucepan, heat the oil to 350°F (175°C). With a wide spatula, slide a few donuts at a time into the hot oil, turning them around as they float to the top. Fry each side of donuts until golden brown. Next, remove fried donuts from hot oil and drain on a wire rack or paper towels.

Note: When frying is finished, let cool slightly. Top with chocolate, sugar, or your preferred ingredients. Enjoy!

Nutrition facts per serving: 198 calories; sodium 171.5mg 7% DV; carbohydrates 15.5g 5% DV; fat 14.3g 22% DV; protein 2.2g 4% DV; cholesterol 14mg 5% DV.

Herman Sourdough Applesauce Donuts

Soft, delicious donuts made with Herman Sourdough Starter. Dust with powdered sugar or cinnamon sugar while still warm.

Total time: 50 minutes

Servings: 12

Yield: 12 donuts

Ingredients:

- ½ teaspoon of baking soda
- ½ cup of white sugar
- 1 tbsp. of water
- 2 tbsp. shortening
- 1/2 cup of Herman Sourdough Starter
- 2 large egg yolks
- 6 cups of vegetable oil for frying
- ½ tsp of vanilla extract
- 1/2 cup of applesauce

- 1/4 cup of buttermilk

- 1/2 tsp of ground cinnamon

- 1/2 tsp of ground nutmeg

- 11/2 tsp of baking powder

- 2 3/4 cups of all-purpose flour

Directions:

- Step one: In a small container, dissolve baking soda in warm water.

- Step two: Combine sugar and shortening in a large bowl. Stir in Herman Sourdough Starter, egg yolks, vanilla extract, applesauce, buttermilk, and the melted baking soda. Set aside. Next, combine nutmeg, cinnamon, baking powder, and flour in a separate bowl. Then, stir in the flour mixture the Sourdough Starter mixture until smooth and firm.

- Step three: Transfer dough into a floured work surface and roll out ¾ inch thick. Next, cut the dough into 12 pieces round shape and then create a hole in the center with a small cutter. Leave the donuts on the floured surface for about 20 minutes for them to rise to double.

- Step four: In a large heavy skillet, deep-fryer, or large saucepan, heat the oil to 350°F (175 degrees C). With a wide spatula, slide a few donuts at a time into the hot oil, turning them around as they float to the top. Fry each side of donuts until golden brown. Next, remove fried donuts from hot oil and drain on a wire rack or paper towels.

Nutritional facts per Serving: 302 calories; carbohydrates 32g 10% DV; protein 3.6g 7% DV; sodium 120.9mg 5% DV; fat 17.9g 28% DV; cholesterol 34.1mg 11% DV.

Sugar Coated Sufganiot

Total time: 1 day

Servings: 24

Yield: 24 donuts

Ingredients:

- 2 1/2 tsp of active dry yeast
- 2 tbsp. of white sugar
- 3/4 cup of warm milk (110°F or 45°C)
- 2 1/2 cups of all-purpose flour
- 1/4 tsp of salt
- 1/4 cup of white sugar
- 2 tbsp. of butter, softened
- 2 large egg yolks
- 1 tsp of ground nutmeg
- 1/2 cup of drained cottage cheese
- 1 egg

- 1 tsp of vanilla extract

- 6 cups of vegetable oil for deep-frying

- 1/2 cup of confectioners' sugar

Directions

- Step one: Dissolve yeast and 2 tbsp. of white sugar in the warm milk and set aside.

- Step two: Place the flour inside a large container and create a hole in the center. Next, add the yeast mixture, butter, nutmeg, egg yolks, salt, and ¼ cup white sugar. After that, stir the flour into the center to combine well. Transfer the dough to a lightly floured work surface and knead the dough until smooth and elastic, about 5 minutes. Cover the dough with a damp cloth in a warm area (room temperature) until it rises overnight.

- Step three: On a floured work surface, roll out dough of ¼ inch thick and cut into 24 2-inch round shape pieces. Next, cover the donuts and let sit for 20 minutes to rise.

- Step four: add the cottage cheese, vanilla, egg, and 3 tbsp. of white sugar in a shallow bowl. Stir the mixture until well combined.

- Step five: Insert 2 tsp of cheese filling into each of the round formed donut.

- Step six: In a large heavy skillet, deep-fryer, or large saucepan, heat the oil to 350°F (175°C). With a wide spatula, slide a few donuts at a time into the hot oil, turning them around as they float to the top. Fry each side of donuts until golden brown. Next, remove fried donuts from hot oil and drain on a wire rack or paper towels. Coat the donuts with confectioners' sugar when still hot. Enjoy!

Nutrition facts per serving: 420 calories; carbohydrates 16.3g 5% DV; protein 2.8g 6% DV; sodium 57.3mg 2% DV; fat 38.8g 60% DV; cholesterol 28.7mg 10% DV.

Sweet French Donuts (Bugnes Moelleuses)

Total: 2 hours 32 minutes

Servings: 24

Yield: 24 donuts

Ingredients:

- 2 (.25 oz.) packages of active dry yeast
- 1/4 cup of warm water
- 8 cups of all-purpose flour
- 3/4 cup of butter, melted
- 8 large eggs
- 2 tbsp. of white sugar
- 1/2 cup white sugar
- 2 lemons, zest
- 6 cups of vegetable oil for deep-frying

Directions:

- Step one: Sprinkle the yeast over 1/4 cup of warm water in a small bowl and let sit until dissolved, about 10 minutes.

- Step two: In a large bowl, combine the flour, butter, white sugar, and lemon zest. Stir the mixture well to combine; stir in the yeast mixture. Next, knead the mixture until the dough is smooth and stretchy. Then, cover the dough with a damp towel and leave to rise to double about two hours.

- Step three: Transfer the dough to a lightly floured surface and roll out a large rectangle. Next, with a small pastry cutter, cut the dough to create diamond shapes.

- Step four: Step five: In a large heavy skillet, deep-fryer, or large saucepan, heat the oil to 350°F (175°C). With a wide spatula, slide a few donuts at a time into the hot oil, turning them around as they float to the top. Fry each side of donuts until golden brown. Next, remove fried donuts from hot oil and drain on a wire rack or paper towels. Coat the donut with your favorite. Enjoy!

Nutrition facts per serving: 297 calories; carbohydrates 37.4g 12% DV; protein 6.7g 13% DV; fat 13.3g 21% DV; sodium 65.4mg 3% DV; cholesterol 77.3mg 26% DV.

Sugar Glazed Donuts

Total time: 2 hours 55 minutes

Servings: 24

Yield: 24 donuts

Ingredients:

- 3/4 cup of scalded milk
- 1/4 tsp of salt
- 1/3cup of granulated sugar
- 1 (.25 oz.) envelope of active dry yeast
- 1/4 cup of warm water
- 4 cups of all-purpose flour
- 1 tsp of grated nutmeg
- 1/3 cup of butter
- 2 large eggs, beaten
- 6 cups of vegetable oil for deep-frying
- 2 cups confectioners' sugar

- 6 tbsp. of milk

Directions:

- Step one: Sprinkle the yeast over 1/4 cup of warm water in a small bowl and let sit until dissolved, about 10 minutes.

- Step two: Combine the scalded milk, salt, and sugar in a small bowl and set aside to cool. Next, add the nutmeg to flour in a large bowl and stir well to combine. Measure 2 cups of the flour mixture and combine it with the milk mixture. Stir thoroughly to combine.

- Step three: Stir the dissolved yeast into the flour and milk mixture. Next, stir in eggs and butter. Stir in the remaining 2 cups of flour half cup a time. Knead the dough until smooth and firm, 5 minutes. Cover the bowl and place it in a warm area until it rises to double about 40 minutes.

- Step four: Transfer the dough to a floured work surface and roll it out to half-inch thick. With a floured donut cutter, cut dough into circles and make a small hole in the center. Let stand to rise for about 30 minutes.

- Step five: In a large heavy skillet, deep-fryer, or large saucepan, heat the oil to 350°F (175°C). With a wide spatula, slide a few donuts at a time into the hot oil, turning them around as they float to the top. Fry each side of donuts until golden brown. Next, remove fried donuts from hot oil and drain on a wire rack or paper towels.

- Step six: To prepare the glaze, combine the 6 tbsp. of milk and confectioners' sugar and stir until smooth. Next, dip warm donuts into glaze and leave to cool a bit. Enjoy!

Nutrition facts per serving: 194 calories; carbohydrates 29.4g 10% DV; protein 3.2g 6% DV; fat 7.1g 11% DV; sodium 53.6mg 2% DV cholesterol 23.2mg 8% DV.

Pumpkin Cranberry Jelly Donuts

(Sufganiot)

Total time: 6 hours 15 minutes

Servings: 18

Yield: 2 1/2 dozen donuts

Ingredients:

- 1/2 cup of unsalted butter
- 1/4 cup of warm milk
- 3/4 cup of white sugar
- 1 cup of canned pumpkin puree
- 1 egg yolk
- 2 large eggs
- 5 cups of all-purpose flour
- 1 (.25 oz.) package of active yeast
- 1/2 tsp of ground cinnamon
- 1 tsp of salt

- 1/2 tsp of ground ginger

- 1/4 tsp of ground nutmeg

- 1/8 tsp of ground allspice

For Filling:

- 1 (14 oz.) can of jellied cranberry sauce

- 1/3 cup of water

- 8 cups of vegetable oil for deep-frying

- 1 egg white

- 1 tsp of water

- 1/2 cup of white sugar, or as needed

- 1/4 cup of confectioners' sugar

Directions:

- Step one: Place the butter in a large bowl and pour the hot milk over it, stirring until butter melts. Next, stir in the ¾ cup of white sugar, pumpkin puree, egg yolk, and eggs into the butter mixture.

- Step two: Combine the flour, yeast, cinnamon, salt, ginger, nutmeg, and allspice in a separate bowl; mix thoroughly until well combined. Next, slowly stir in the flour mixture to the milk mixture; mix until smooth. The dough will be very wet, almost cookie-dough consistency; do not bother; it will absorb moisture as it stands for a while.

- Step three: Place the dough in a greased bowl and cover with a damp plastic wrap. Next, Place in the refrigerator for about five hours or overnight.

- Step four: In a small pot over medium-low heat, combine the cranberry sauce with ⅓ cup of water. Heat the mixture for about 25 minutes or until cranberry sauce melts, stirring occasionally. Remove from heat, pour into a container and refrigerate.

- Step five: Transfer the dough to a lightly floured work surface. Next, mold the dough into a ball shape, divide it into two, then return one part of the dough to the greased bowl. Cover with a plastic wrap and refrigerate. After that, roll out the remaining half dough on a lightly floured surface to ¼ inch thick. Use a dough cutter to cut out dough rounds.

- Step six: Line a baking sheet with a silicone liner or parchment paper. Next, transfer the dough rounds to the baking sheet in pairs (one will be the bottom half while the other will be the top half of the donuts).

- Step seven: beat the egg white with one tsp of water in a small bowl. Next, brush the bottom half of the dough rounds with the beaten egg white and then scoop one tsp of cranberry jelly into the center of each bottom round. Next, place the top dough rounds and press to be sealed. Leave the donuts to sit for about 20 minutes.

- Step eight: In a large heavy skillet, deep-fryer, or large saucepan, heat the oil to 350°F (175°C). With a wide spatula, slide a few donuts at a time into the hot oil, turning them around as they float to the top. Fry each side of donuts until golden brown. Next, remove fried donuts from hot oil and drain on a wire rack or paper towels. Coat the donuts with sugar while still warm and dust with the confectioners' sugar. Enjoy!

Nutrition Facts per Serving: 316 calories; carbohydrates 49.4g 16% DV; protein 5.1g 10% DV; sodium 217.2mg 9% DV; fat 11.1g 17% DV; cholesterol 46.4mg 16% DV

Thera's Canadian Donuts

Total time: 2 hours 5 minutes

Servings: 20

Yield: 20 pastries

Ingredients:

- 1/2 cup of warm water (110°F/45°C)
- 5 tsp of active dry yeast
- 1 pinch of white sugar
- 1/3 cup of white sugar
- 1 cup of warm milk (110°F/45°C)
- 1 tsp of vanilla extract
- 1 1/2 tsp of salt
- 3 large eggs, beaten
- 1/3 cup of vegetable oil
- 5 cups of whole-wheat flour, divided
- 6 cups of vegetable oil for frying

- 1/2 tsp of ground cinnamon, or to taste

- 2 cups of white sugar

Directions:

- Step one: Dissolve 1 pinch of sugar in the warm water. Sprinkle yeast over it and let sit until yeast starts foaming, about 5 minutes. Next, add the ⅓ cup of sugar, warm milk, vanilla extract, salt, eggs, and ⅓ cup of oil; stir the mixture until sugar dissolved. Then, slowly add 21/2 cup of the flour, stir well until dough is too firm. Transfer the dough to a floured work surface; knead in more flour until dough is smooth and stretchy. Mold the dough into a ball shape, transfer to a greased bowl; cover the bowl and leave for about one hour to rise to double.

- Step two: Return the dough to the work surface, knead again to reshape, and roll out the dough into oval shapes {about an egg size} of ¼ inch thick. Make 20 pieces of pastry.

- Step three: In a shallow bowl, combine cinnamon with 2 cups of white sugar to taste and set aside.

- Step four: In a large heavy skillet, deep-fryer, or large saucepan, heat the oil to 350°F (175°C). With a wide spatula, slide a few pastries at a time into the hot oil, turning them around as they float to the top. Fry each side of pastries until golden brown. Next, remove fried pastries from hot oil and drain on a wire rack or paper towels. To serve, dip the pastry into the cinnamon mixture when still warm. And then shake off excess sugar. Enjoy!

Nutrition facts per serving: 284 calories; carbohydrates 46.2g 15% DV; protein 5.8g 12% DV; fat 9.7g 15% DV; sodium 192.1mg 8% DV; cholesterol 28.9mg 10% DV

Vanilla Glazed Creamy Donuts

Total time: 3 hours

Serving: 12

Yield: 12 donuts

Ingredients:

For Donuts:

- 1 1/4 cups of warm milk
- 2 1/4 tsp (one package) of active dry yeast
- 2 eggs, beaten
- 8 tbsp. of butter, melted and cooled
- 1/4 cup of granulated sugar
- 1 tsp of salt
- 4 1/4 cups of all-purpose flour
- 6 cups of oil for deep-frying

For Glaze:

- 1/4 cup of unsweetened cocoa powder

- 1 3/4 cups of powdered sugar
- 1 tsp of vanilla
- 1/4 cup of milk
- For the Pastry Cream:
- 2 tbsp. of flour
- 2/3 cup of sugar
- 2 tbsp. of cornstarch
- 1 pinch of salt
- 2 eggs
- 2 cups of cream
- 2 tbsp. of softened unsalted butter
- 2 tsp of vanilla

Directions:

- Step one: In a large bowl, combine the milk and the yeast; stir the mixture gently for about five minutes or until foamy. Next, stir in the butter, egg, salt and sugar into the yeast mixture. Slowly stir in half of the flour and mix well to combine. After that, add the remaining flour, a little at a time, and mix until dough is firm.

- Step two: Transfer the dough to a lightly floured surface and knead until smooth and stretchy. Next, transfer the dough to a greased bowl, cover with a damp towel, and set aside for 1 hour to rise until double in size.

- Step three: Return the dough to the lightly floured work surface; roll the dough out to half-inch thick. With a floured 3 inches donut cutter, cut into 12 pieces. Make a hole if desired. Cover the donuts with a damp towel and let sit in a warm area for about 40 minutes until it rises again.

- Step four: In a large heavy skillet, deep-fryer, or large saucepan, heat the oil to 350°F (175°C). With a wide spatula, slide a few pastries at a time into the hot oil, turning them around as they float to the top. Fry each side of pastries until golden brown. Next, remove fried pastries from hot oil and drain on a wire rack or paper towels.

For the Glaze:

In a small bowl, beat the cocoa powder, powdered sugar, vanilla, and milk until very smooth. Next, dip the top of each donut in the glaze and return to the wire rack to harden.

For the Pastry Cream Filling:

Place a small saucepan over medium heat; add the flour, sugar, cornstarch, and salt. Next, stir in the cream and eggs. Bring the mixture to a boil, while stirring constantly, keep boiling for about 10 minutes until thickened. Reduce heat, so the mixture boils gently; continue cooking until the mixture coats the back of a spoon. Next, stir in the vanilla and butter. Strain the cream filling through a fine-mesh sieve and let cool before using.

To serve, poke holes into the side of the donuts with a chopstick or funnel and insert the pastry cream as you desire. Enjoy!

Jelly Filled Yummy Donuts

You are free to use jelly, Jam, Marmalade, or whatever you prefer that tastes good. This will replace the fluorescent red, sickly sweet jelly that donut shops tend to rely on.

Total time: 3 hours

Yield: 12 donuts

Servings: 12

Ingredients:

- 1 1/4 cups of warm milk
- 2 1/4 tsp (one package) of active dry yeast
- 8 tbsp. of butter, melted and cooled
- 2 eggs, beaten
- 1/4 cup of granulated sugar
- 1 tsp of salt
- 4 1/4 cups of all-purpose flour
- 6 cups of vegetable oil for frying

Directions:

- Step one: In a large bowl, combine the milk and the yeast; stir the mixture gently for about five minutes or until foamy. Next, stir in the butter, egg, salt and sugar into the yeast mixture. Slowly stir in half of the flour and mix well to combine. After that, add the remaining flour, a little at a time, and mix until dough is firm.

- Step two: Transfer the dough to a lightly floured surface and knead until smooth and stretchy. Next, transfer the dough to a greased bowl, cover with a damp towel and set aside for 1 hour to rise until double in size.

- Step three: Return the dough to the lightly floured work surface; roll the dough out to half-inch thick. With a floured donut cutter, cut into about 3 inches each. Make a hole if desired. Cover the donuts with a kitchen towel and let sit in a warm area for about 40 minutes until it rises again.

- Step four: In a large heavy skillet, deep-fryer, or large saucepan, heat the oil to 350°F (175°C). With a wide spatula, slide a few donuts at a time into the hot oil, turning them around as they float to the top. Fry each side of donuts until golden brown. Next, remove fried donuts from hot oil and drain on a wire rack or paper towels.

To serve, insert a funnel into each donut's side and fill the jelly into the middle. Enjoy!

Nutritional fact per serving: 313 calories; 40 grams carbohydrates; 7 grams protein; 14 grams fat; 2 grams saturated fat; 8 grams monounsaturated fat; 4 grams polyunsaturated fat; 216 milligrams sodium; 1 gram dietary fiber; 6 grams sugars

Costas French Donuts (Beignets)

Total time: 1 hour 30 minutes

Servings: 12

Yield: 12 donuts

Ingredients:

- 2 (.25 oz.) packages of active dry yeast
- 1/2 cup of warm water
- 1/2 cup of sugar
- 1/4 cup of shortening
- 1 tsp of salt
- 1 cup of hot water
- 1 cup of evaporated milk
- 2 large eggs, beaten
- 7 1/2 cups of flour
- 8 cups of vegetable oil for deep-frying
- 1 cup of confectioners' sugar

Directions:

- Step one: Sprinkle yeast over the warm water in a small mixing bowl and let sit until dissolved, about 10 minutes.

- Step two: In a large bowl, combine the sugar, shortening, and salt. Next, pour the warm water over the sugar mixture, add the evaporated milk, and stir well to combine. Let the mixture stand to cool a bit. After that, add the beaten eggs and yeast mixture.

- Step three: Slowly stir in the flour to the wet ingredients and mix until smooth and stretchy. Next, cover the dough with a damp towel and leave to rise or refrigerate for about one hour.

- Step four: Transfer the dough into a lightly floured work surface and roll out the dough to 1/4 inch thick. Next, cut the dough into strips of about 3 inches wide, and then cut again to create diamond shapes.

- Step five: In a large heavy skillet, deep-fryer, or large saucepan, heat the oil to 350°F (175°C). With a wide spatula, slide a few donuts at a time into the hot oil, turning them around as they float to the top. Fry each side of donuts until golden brown. Next, remove fried donuts from hot oil and drain on a wire rack or paper towels. Coat the donuts with confectioners' sugar when still hot. Enjoy!

Nutrition facts per serving: 503 calories; carbohydrates 80.9g 26% DV; protein 10.9g 22% DV; fat 14.8g 23% DV; sodium 230.8mg 9% DV; cholesterol 37.1mg 12% DV.

Sweet Donuts with Apple Cider

Yield: About: 24 donuts

Serving: 24

Total time: 40 minutes

Ingredients:

- 1 cup of apple cider
- 1 tsp of baking soda
- 1 1/2 tsp of baking powder
- 1/4 tsp of freshly grated nutmeg
- 1/4 tsp of salt
- 1 1/2 tsp of ground cinnamon
- 4 tsp of unsalted butter
- 1/4 cup of packed brown sugar
- 1 1/2 cups of granulated sugar
- 1 tsp of vanilla extract
- 2 large eggs, beaten

- 1/2 cup of buttermilk

- 5 1/2 cups of all-purpose flour

- 1 medium Honey crisp apple or other tart cooking apple, peeled and cut into ¼ inch cube.

- 8 cups of vegetable oil for deep-frying

- Blueberry ginger jam for serving, optional

Directions:

- Step one: Place a small pot over high heat; pour the apple cider and boil until it reduces to ½ cup; turn off the heat and set aside.

- Step two: Combine the flour, baking soda, baking powder, nutmeg, salt, and ½ tsp of the cinnamon and set aside.

- Step three: Combine the butter, brown sugar, and 1 cup of granulated sugar until smooth in an electric mixer fitted with a paddle. Next, mix in the vanilla, egg, buttermilk, and apple cider.

- Step four: Scrape down bowl and add the flour. Next, mix until well combined, and then remove the bowl from the mixer. Add the Honey crisp apple and use your hand to mix until blended. Cover and place in the refrigerator for 30 minutes

- Step five: Transfer the dough into a floured work surface and roll out round shapes donuts about ½ inch thick and then make holes in the center. Next, combine the remaining 1 tsp of cinnamon and ½ cup of sugar.

- Step six: In a large heavy skillet, deep-fryer, or large saucepan, heat the oil to 350°F (175°C). With a wide spatula, slide a few donuts at a time into the hot oil, turning them around as they float to the top. Fry each side of donuts until golden brown. Next, remove fried donuts from hot oil and drain on a wire rack or paper towels. Coat the donuts in cinnamon sugar while still warm. Serve with blueberry ginger jam for spreading or dipping if desired. Enjoy!

Nutritional analysis per serving: 291 calories; 2 grams saturated fat; 8 grams monounsaturated fat; 13 grams fat; 2 grams polyunsaturated fat; 39 grams carbohydrates; 4 grams protein; 117 milligrams sodium;1 gram dietary fiber; 17 grams sugar.

Portuguese Delicious Donuts

(Malasadas Dois)

Total time: 1 day

Servings: 24

Yield: 24 servings

Ingredients:

- 1 tsp of sugar
- 1/4 cup of warm water
- 1 (.25 oz.) envelope of active dry yeast
- 4 large eggs
- 1 tsp of salt
- 4 cups of all-purpose flour
- 1 cup of white sugar
- 3/4 cup melted butter
- 1 cup of lukewarm milk

- 8 cups vegetable oil for deep-frying
- 1 cup of white sugar for coating

Directions:

- Step one: Dissolve 1 tsp of sugar in ¼ cups of warm water. Sprinkle yeast over it and leave for 5 minutes to dissolve.

- Step two: Stir the eggs and one cup of sugar in a large bowl until sugar dissolved. Next, add salt and flour, stirring with a wooden spoon until smooth. Stir in the yeast mixture, melted butter, and milk. Next, knead the dough until smooth and stretchy, 5 minutes. Cover the bowl and place it in a warm area until it rises to double.

- Step three: Transfer the dough to a floured work surface and roll it out to half-inch thick. Next, cut the dough into 24 pieces' ball and leave the donuts to rise again until double. Use a damp cloth to cover loosely.

- Step four: Stretch each ball to form a round shape of about 4 inches wide, and then create a hole in the center with a small cutter. Leave the donuts loosely covered on the floured surface for about 40 minutes for them to rise.

- Step five: In a large heavy skillet, deep-fryer, or large saucepan, heat the oil to 350°F (175°C). With a wide spatula, slide a few donuts at a time into the hot oil, turning them around as they float to the top. Fry each side of donuts until golden brown. Next, remove fried donuts from hot oil and drain on a wire rack or paper towels. Coat the donuts with white sugar when still warm. Enjoy!

Nutrition facts per serving: 121 calories; carbohydrates 16.6g 5% DV; protein 1.9g 4% DV; cholesterol 23.5mg 8% DV; fat 5.3g 8% DV; sodium 77.1mg 3% DV.

Quick & Easy Ricotta Donuts

This is a delicious dessert or breakfast recipe made with ricotta cheese. It's an easy and quick mini donut.

Total time: 15 minutes

Yield: 12 donuts

Servings:12

Ingredients:

- 350 grams of ricotta or fresh farmer's cheese
- 2 1/2 cups of all-purpose flour
- 1/2 cup of sugar
- 2 tsp of baking powder
- 1 large egg
- 4 egg yolks can be replaced with 1 whole egg
- 1/4 tsp of salt
- 6 cups of oil for deep-frying
- Chocolate ganache or powdered sugar for serving

Directions:

- Step one: in a large bowl, combine the ricotta, flour, sugar, baking powder, egg and egg yolks, and salt. Mix the ingredients thoroughly with your mixer paddle attachment or by hand to combine well. Add more egg to bring it together if the mixture feels too dry.

- Step two: Transfer the dough into a floured work surface, roll it out 1-inch-thick, and cut out 12 pieces of 2 inch round donuts with a donut cutter.

- Step three: In a large heavy skillet, deep-fryer, or large saucepan, heat the oil to 350°F (175°C). With a wide spatula, slide a few donuts at a time into the hot oil, turning them around as they float to the top. Fry each side of donuts until golden brown. Next, remove fried donuts from hot oil and drain on a wire rack or paper towels. Coat the donuts with sugar while still warm.

Note: You can serve this delicious donut with chocolate ganache on the side or serve with just powdered sugar. Enjoy with your favorite drink!

Nutrition Facts per serving: Calories 199 Calories; Carbohydrates 28g9%; Fat 5g8%; Saturated Fat 3g19%; Cholesterol 93mg31%; Protein 7g14%Sodium 82mg4%; Potassium 153mg4%; Sugar 8g9%; Vitamin A 235IU5%; Calcium 110mg11%; Iron 1.6mg9%

Sugar Glazed Super Soft Donuts

These DIY donut recipes are very soft yet crispy topped with a powdered sugar glaze.

Total time: 1 hour 50 minutes

Servings: 15

Yield: About 15 donuts

Ingredients:

- 1 cup of warm milk
- 1 egg, beaten
- 2 tsp of dry instant yeast
- 1/2 cup of sugar
- 1 tsp of salt
- 3 1/2 cups of all-purpose flour
- 1/4 cup butter, warmed
- 6 cups of oil for deep-frying
- 1/4 cup water or whole milk

- 2 cups powdered/confectioner's sugar

Directions:

- Step one: In bread making machine or mixer, add the milk, beaten egg, yeast, ½ cup sugar, salt, and flour. Next, turn the machine into a dough circle. Next, add the warm butter 10 minutes before the completion of the dough circle. Do not open the lid when the dough circle is complete so that warm air doesn't escape. Let the mixture sits in the bread machine for 1 hour to rise to double. For the mixer, begin with the lowest speed; add the butter and then increase speed 1-2 numbers; use a dough hook and knead for 20 minutes. Next, transfer it to a greased large bowl, cover the bowl with plastic wrap, and let sit in a warm place for 2 hours to double in size.

- Step two: Transfer the dough into a lightly floured work surface and shape it into a ball and let rest for 10 minutes.

- Step three: Transfer the dough to a lightly floured work surface and roll it out to a ½ inch thick with a floured rolling pin. Next, cut out 3 inch round donuts with a 3-inch cookie cutter and then create a hole in the center.

- Step four: In a large heavy skillet, deep-fryer, or large saucepan, heat the oil to 350°F (175°C). With a wide spatula, slide a few donuts at a time into the hot oil, turning them around as they float to the top. Fry each side of donuts until golden brown. Next, remove fried donuts from hot oil and drain on a wire rack or paper towels.

- Step five: For the sugar glaze, Mix ¼ cup of milk or water and the powdered sugar. Next, whisk the mixture until well combined. Add more milk or water if you prefer a thinner glaze, or add more sugar if you want a thicker glaze. Dip each donut inside the glaze and set over the rack. Enjoy!

Printed in Great Britain
by Amazon